THE OFFICIAL

YOU ARE MY BORO

ANNUAL 2010

A-Z & 1-Eleven

Written by Graham Bell

This book belongs to Daniel Calvert

Age 12

Favourite player Adam Johnson

Prediction of Boro's final position this season

Prediction of Coca-Cola Championship winners this season

Prediction of FA Cup winners this season

Prediction of Carling Cup winners this season

Prediction of teams to be promoted to the Barclays Premier League this season

1st

2nd

Play Off Winners

A TWOCAN PUBLICATION

©2009. Published by Twocan under licence from Middlesbrough FC

ISBN 978-0-9559299-4-6

PICTURE CREDITS
Getty Images, Blades Sports Photography, Hawes Gate Photography, North News & Pictures.

£7

YOU ARE MY BORO

MIDDLESBROUGH
FOOTBALL CLUB
1876
YOU ARE MY BORO

CONTENTS

A

The stunning new adidas 2009-10 home shirt modelled by star defenders David Wheater and Tony McMahon features a white sash on both sides of a red shirt plus the famous adidas stripes down both shoulders.

The shirts feature adidas Climacool fabric, an integrated system of technologies to regulate the wearer's body temperature, take sweat away from the body and allow air to circulate close to the skin.

THE BEAUTIFUL GAME

It will be the first time for a decade that Boro have worn white shorts, while white socks make a comeback for the first time since the unforgettable 1995-96 season when Juninho made his first appearance at the new Riverside Stadium.

JUNINHO

JUNINHO SKIPPING PAST BORO LEGEND GARY PALLISTER

Boro also wore white socks when Boro last carried adidas branding back in 1982-83.

Arsenal 0 Boro 1

Tuesday January 20 2004

It took a touch of Brazilian magic to light up a damp North London night and leave Boro one foot in what would be a historic Carling Cup final.

Juninho almost put Boro in front with 15 minutes played before Massimo Maccarone also went close. But seven minutes into the second half, Juninho's low drive whistled past Arsenal keeper Graham Stack to earn Boro a 1-0 win.

Determination from Franck Queudrue saw him maintain possession and lay the ball to Gaizka Mendieta. The Spanish international kept calm as he was closed down on the D, rolling the ball to Juninho, who ghosted in unmarked on the left of the area and fired low into the bottom corner.

Boro won the second leg 2-1 two weeks later to reach the final, where they triumphed 2-1 against Bolton.

ARSENAL: Stack; Toure, Cygan, Keown (Captain), Clichy, Parlour, Edu, Gilberto, Bentley (Smith 73), Kanu, Quincy (Thomas 63).
Unused subs: Holloway (gk); Cole, Skulason.

MIDDLESBROUGH: Schwarzer; Mills, Ehiogu (Captain), Riggott, Queudrue, Mendieta (Parnaby 80), Boateng, Doriva, Zenden, Juninho, Maccarone (Job 77).
Unused subs: Jones (gk); Downing, Ricketts.

ARSENAL'S GAEL CLICHY CHASES GAIZKA MENDIETA

JUNINHO JINKS AWAY FROM KOLO TOURE

ONE FOR THE road

BORO TRAVEL IN STYLE

Boro's new-look adidas change strip for the 2009-2010 campaign features a cyan shirt, shorts and socks with the unmistakeable adidas stripes.

C

Crest test

Can you name the Championship teams that these Crests belong to?

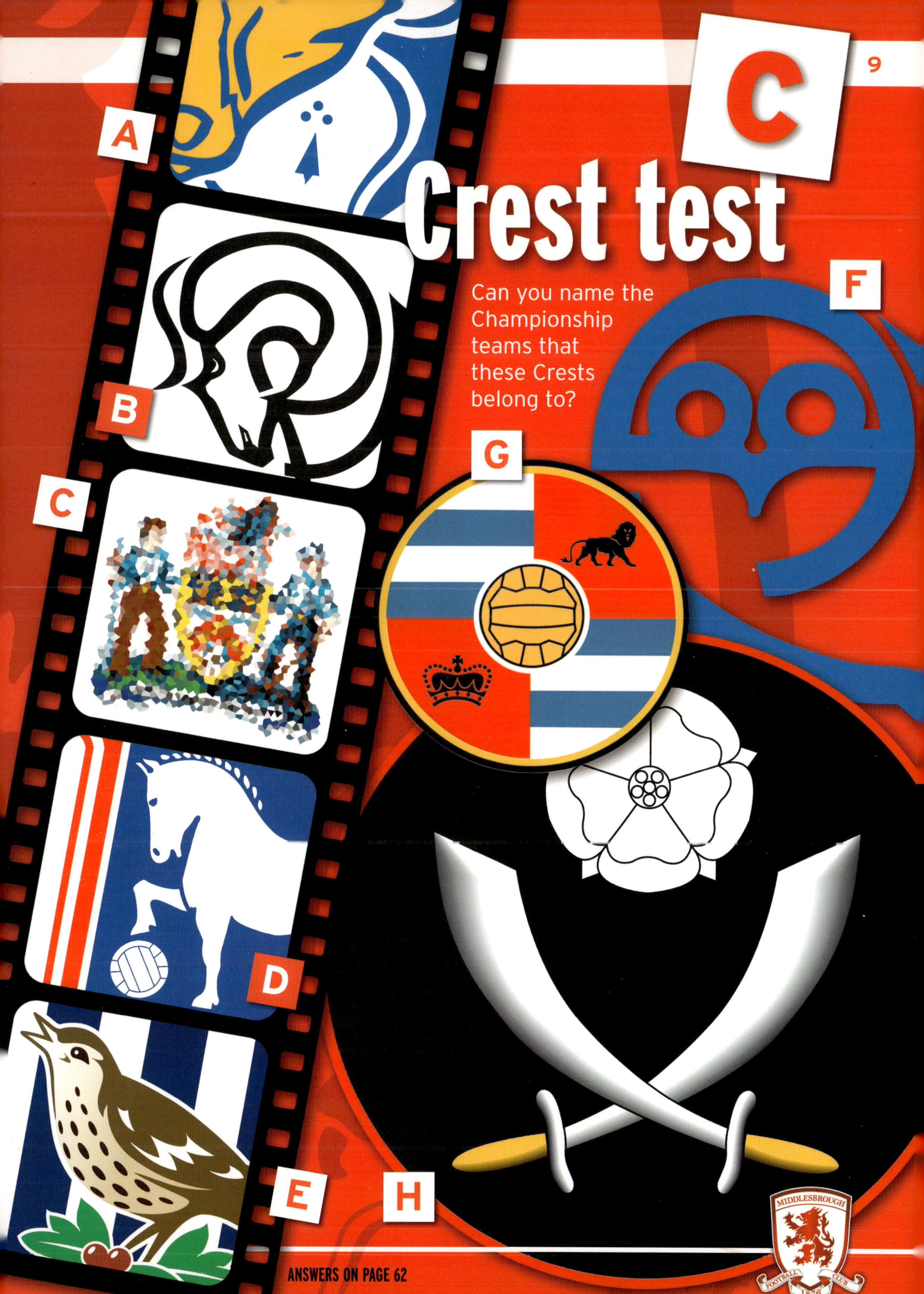

ANSWERS ON PAGE 62

C

CLASS

OF 09·10

MARK Yeates

FIVE INTERESTING FACTS ABOUT MARK

1. Mark became the first senior player from outside the top two divisions to join Boro since Craig Hignett's £500,000 transfer from Crewe in November 1992. **2.** A free-kick specialist and although he is primarily right-footed, he has also struck a number of spectacular goals with his left. His favourite goal scored was a free-kick from a seemingly impossible angle in a 2-1 Colchester victory against Leeds Utd at Elland Road on Dec 13 2008. **3.** He went on a blistering run of seven goals in nine games for Colchester after their promotion to the Championship. However, his season was cruelly cut short by a dislocated shoulder and he was forced to sit out the final three months as United were relegated. **4.** Mark, who played nearly 4,000 minutes of football for Colchester last year, is 5ft 9ins tall and weighs 10st 7lbs. **5.** He joins the list of Dublin-born Boro stars that includes Arthur Fitzsimons, Jimmy Hartnett, Alan Moore, Jason Gavin, Curtis Fleming, Michael Cummins, Keith O'Halloran and Keith O'Neill.

7 **DATE OF BIRTH:** January 11 1985 **NATIONALITY:** Irish
FORMER CLUBS: Tottenham Hotspur, Swindon Town, Colchester United, Hull City, Leicester City

LEROY Lita

FIVE INTERESTING FACTS ABOUT LEROY

1. Born in Kinshasa, in the Democratic Republic of Congo, Leroy moved to England when he was five. He remembers playing football barefoot in the streets of Kinshasa, where he says "life was hard". **2.** Leroy was on Chelsea's books as a schoolboy and has special memories of training with the first team stars, including future Boro striker Jimmy Floyd Hasselbaink, who gave him advice on his finishing skills. **3.** He scored 29 goals for Bristol City in 2004-05 - and then scored on his England Under-21 debut against Holland to take his season's total to 30. **4.** Leroy ruined Gareth Southgate's first game as Boro manager by scoring the winner as newly-promoted Reading came from 2-0 down to win 3-2 at the Madejski Stadium in August 2006. **5.** He is a black belt in the Korean martial art of taekwondo.

9 **DATE OF BIRTH:** December 28 1984 **NATIONALITY:** British
FORMER CLUBS: Bristol City, Reading, Charlton Athletic, Norwich City

BACK ROW: Martin Scott (Reserve Team Coach), Marvin Emnes, Tuncay Sanli, Matthew Bates, David Wheater, Seb Hines, Tony McMahon, John Johnson, Afonso Alves, Nathan Porritt, Chris Moseley (Senior Physiotherapist). **MIDDLE ROW:** Steve Pears (Goalkeeping Coach), Jonathan Franks, Josh Walker, Joe Bennett, Richard Smallwood, Robert Huth, Jason Steele, Brad Jones, Danny Coyne, Jonathan Grounds, Rhys Williams, Andrew Taylor, Adam Johnson, Leroy Lita, Adam Reed (Physio). **FRONT ROW:** Nick Allamby (Conditioning Coach), Julio Arca, Justin Hoyte, Mark Yeates, Steve Agnew (Coach), Gareth Southgate (Manager), Colin Cooper (Coach), Emanuel Pogatetz, Didier Digard, Mohamed Shawky, Alan Smith (Football Consultant).

2

Preston defender Sean St Ledger arrived on a three-month loan in September with a possible permanent deal to follow in January.

Born in Birmingham, St Ledger has earned a fine reputation during a career that has taken him from Peterborough to Preston and into the Republic of Ireland's World Cup squad.

After making 79 league appearances for Peterborough, he joined Preston in 2006, where he has gone on to play another 130 league games, scoring seven goals.

He made his full international debut against Nigeria in May and has since won further caps against Bulgaria, Australia, Cyprus and South Africa. He celebrates his 25th birthday three days after Christmas.

...MORE FOR THE pack

DANNY Coyne

FIVE INTERESTING FACTS ABOUT DANNY

1. Danny kept 20 clean sheets for Tranmere Rovers last season to win Coca-Cola League One's Puma Golden Glove prize. No other keeper outside the top flight recorded more shutouts. 2. He joins the list of Welsh internationals to play for the Boro that includes Bobby Atherton, Bert Davis, Love Jones, Freddy Warren, Tom Griffiths, Bill Harris, Mel Nurse, John Mahoney, Clayton Blackmore and a player who once challenged him for the Wales number one jersey, Mark Crossley. 3. Has a happy habit of saving important penalties, including Jack Lester's last-minute spot kick in Tranmere's 2-1 FA Cup win at Chesterfield in Nov 2007. 4. At 35 years old he is by far the oldest player at the club, being seven years older than the previous father of the squad, 28-year-old Chris Riggott. 5. He has won 16 caps for Wales and played in the historic first ever football international at Dublin's Croke Park, which had until recently staged only Gaelic games.

21

DATE OF BIRTH: August 27 1973 **NATIONALITY:** Welsh
FORMER CLUBS: Tranmere Rovers (twice), Grimsby Town, Leicester City, Burnley

TOP 10 DEFENDING TIPS

...are you man enough?

DAVID WHEATER

So, if you think you're up to the job, here are some top tips to get you on your way to becoming a defensive dynamo!

1 **APPLY PRESSURE!** Badger the attacking side constantly to force them to make mistakes, make life as difficult as you can for them. It's hard to score goals when you're under pressure.

2 **BE ON THE BALL!** Stay on your toes and be ready to sprint for a stray ball at any time.

3 **MARK YOUR MAN!** Always know where your attacker is, never let him get behind you or you'll lose sight of the ball.

4 **KEEP YOUR EYES ON THE PRIZE.** Don't let the ball out of your sight, that way, it can't sneak up on you! Also, watch your attacker's feet to anticipate what they will do next.

5 **KEEP IN TOUCH WITH YOUR GOALIE.** He often has a better view of what is going on on the pitch and will be able to direct you.

6 **DON'T DIVE WRECKLESSLY!** If you haven't got a good view of the ball, don't dive or slide in, you'll only get yourself into bother.

7 **NEVER GIVE UP!** Keep moving, if an attacker has gotten past you... go after him, fast!

8 **BE TOUGH!** Tackle hard and fast, but always go for the ball, not the player.

9 **WATCH THE GAME!** Be aware of what's going on and watch for passes you can intercept.

10 **WORK AS A TEAM!** If a fellow defender is working on an attacker, be there to support him. You need to be around to provide back-up if the attacker gets past him.

ONY McMAHON

GARY PALLISTER

Can you identify the eight Boro Stars below?

E STARS IN THEIR eyes

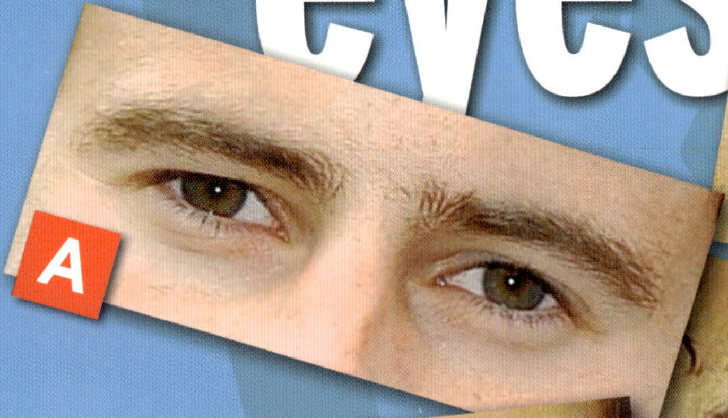
A

B

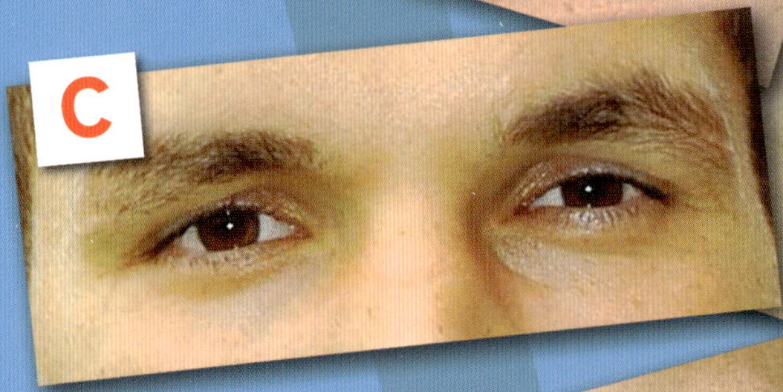
C

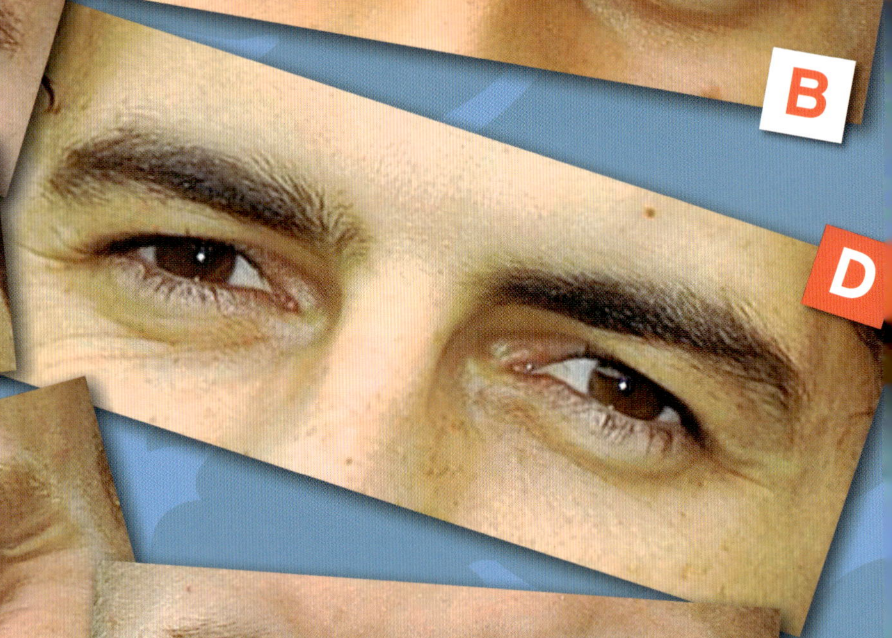
D

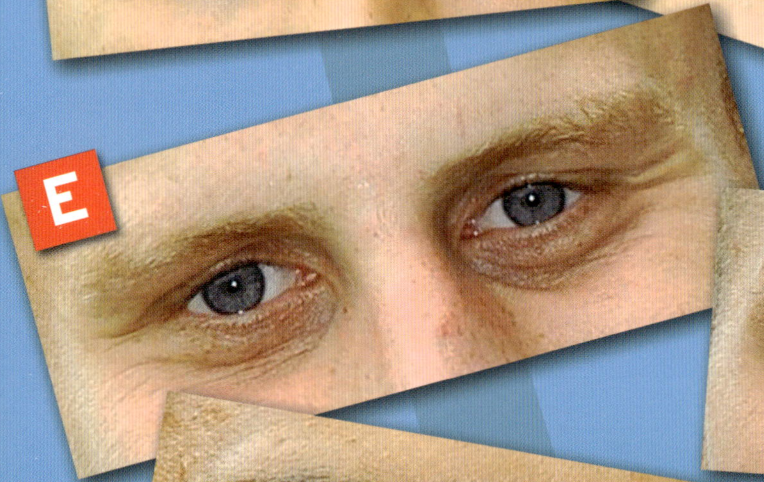
E

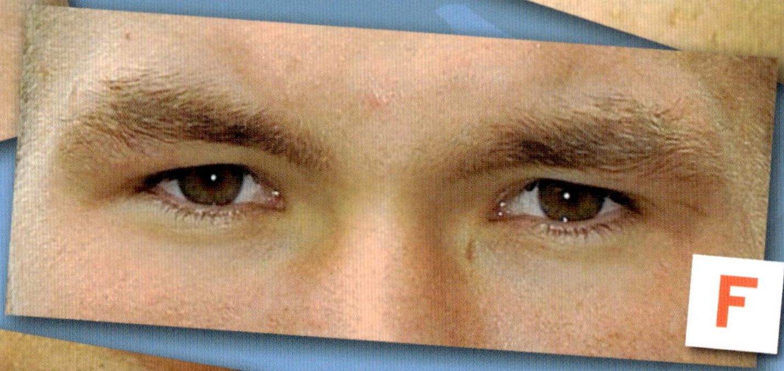
F

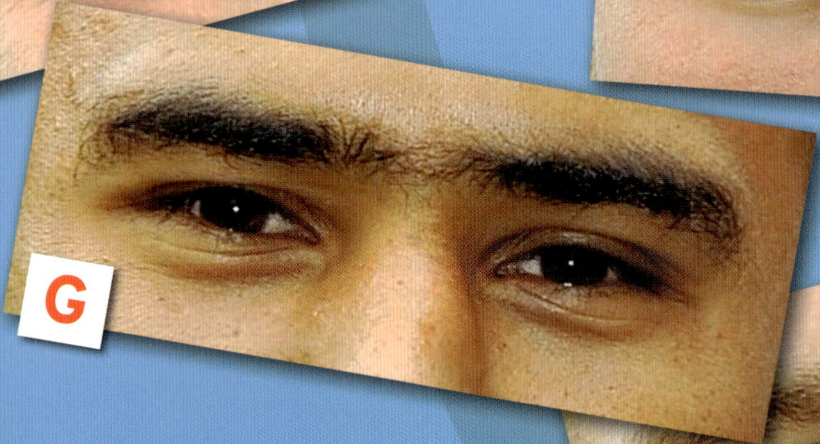
G

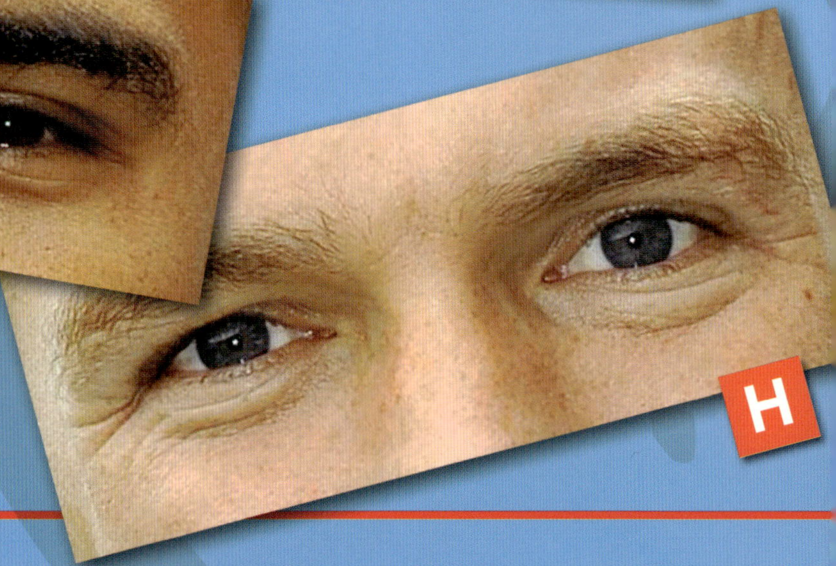
H

ANSWERS ON PAGE 62

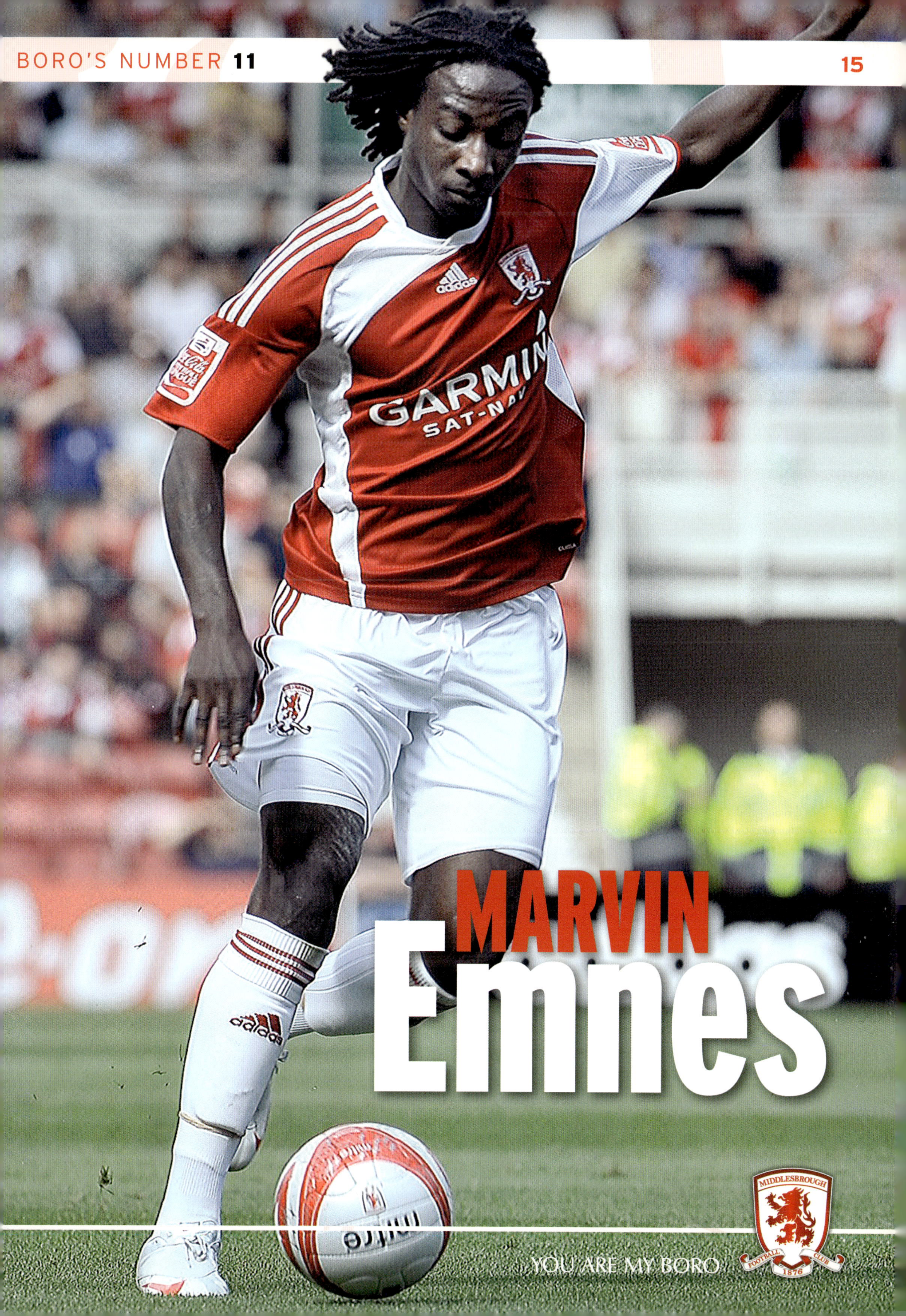

MARVIN Emnes

F

There are five famous sportsmen hidden in the crowd...

FANTASTIC

ANSWERS ON PAGE 62

G

The Gaffer prepares for the match...

I know how much the fans look forward to matches, but perhaps many do not realise the preparation that goes into 90 minutes of football.

The Boro management team and players start our planning weeks ahead and try to leave nothing to chance. Our first priority is to arrive at the ground, whether home or away, in the best physical shape for the challenge ahead.

A lot of football knocks and strains are unavoidable, but our medical department works very hard on injury prevention. If a player has a known physical weakness, perhaps caused by a previous injury, he does extra work before and after training to make his body stronger and more resilient.

All managers want to be able to pick their best players, and time spent on stretching and weights can often avoid spells on the treatment table.

We also spend a lot of time on match analysis, watching tapes of our games to identify strengths and weaknesses. For example, we can see how effective we are at free-kicks and corners, whether we need to improve our marking when defending set-pieces and how we can make our attacking play more effective.

The players are encouraged to have their say, too, and we also make them aware of the opposition's strengths and weaknesses.

Matches also involve a lot of work for backroom staff such as our kitroom. We prepare for away games like an army on the march, with skips full of home or away strips, training gear, food, water and energy drinks.

If it is an away match, there are often flights and hotels to book. Timetables have to be drawn up and training schedules adjusted accordingly.

It's all about being well prepared and professional. And those are qualities we also aim to take on to the pitch.

THE

GAFFER
MIDDLESBROUGH
FOOTBALL CLUB
1876

HEALTHY eating...

Players are able to choose from a range of tasty dishes at Rockliffe Park training ground where a team of cooks ensure they are properly refuelled after hard sessions.

Favourites include chicken, a wide variety of fish, lean meat, pasta and rice. Breakfasts feature cereals, toast and boiled and scrambled eggs.

Each player has a range of foods and products he is advised to choose from. Boro's chefs ensure that they use healthy cooking ingredients such as olive oil and that the food is not too spicy.

After the match it is important to ensure the players eat the right balance of carbohydrate and protein. This is needed to replenish their energy reserves and aid recovery.

Just as important is what the players drink. They use performance-boosting energy drinks and gels and make sure they stay well hydrated at all times.

The days are gone when players wolfed down steak and chips before a match. These days the emphasis is on foods that are easily digested, taste good and increase performances rather than waistlines.

SAMPLE
TRAINING DAY MENU
AT ROCKLIFFE PARK

Leek and Potato Soup

•

Lemon Peppered Chicken
Oriental Pork Stir Fry
Baked Mahi Mahi
Spinach and Ricotta Tortellini
Over Baked Chicken

•

Jacket Potatoes
Roasted Wedges
Broccoli
Peas and Sweetcorn

•

Spicy Tomato Sauce

MIDDLESBROUGH FOOTBALL CLUB 1876
YOU ARE MY BORO

SAMPLE
PRE-MATCH MENU
Pasta
Rice
Lean Chicken
Fish
Potatoes
Vegetables
YOU ARE MY BORO
MIDDLESBROUGH FOOTBALL CLUB 1876
GARMIN SAT-NAV

Internationals

So long the understudy to Mark Schwarzer, Jones emerged as No 1 keeper in the 2008-09 season after fighting off the claims of Ross Turnbull

Williams can play all along the back four and in central midfield. He enjoyed a highly-successful loan spell at Burnley last season and helped them win promotion to the Premier League.

EMANUEL POGATETZ

Appointed club captain at the start of the 2008-2009 season, Pogatetz joined Boro from Bayer Leverkusen in 2005 and is equally effective as a central defender and full-back.

Coyne is the first player to sign for Boro from Tranmere Rovers since Steve Vickers in December 1993.

The midfielder has won more than 60 caps for Egypt and has also celebrated African Nations Cup success with his country

JULIO Arca

...have their own club, the...

BORO JUNIOR LIONS!

You can join the brand new Boro Junior Lions club for the 2009-10 season for just £10 - and Roary's got a whole season's worth of fun ahead for all his members!

Our membership pack is full of great, exclusive competitions, plus you'll get your very own membership card and a certificate from Boro defender David Wheater.

As a special bonus, you'll also receive a brilliant activity gift such as a boomerang, yo-yo or pen torch in the post.

But that's not all!

This year, we are able to offer the following to all our members:

- **A CHRISTMAS CARD**
- **FREE ENTRY INTO HOME RESERVE GAMES**
- **THE CHANCE TO BE A BORO MASCOT**

If you would like to join Boro Junior Lions:

please call: 0844 499 6789
email: borojuniorlions@mfc.co.uk
or visit: www.mfc.co.uk

TOP 10 KEEPING TIPS

BRAD JONES

...but someone's got to do it.

So, if you think you're man enough for the challenge, here are some top tips to get you on track for becoming an all star keeper!

1 **KEEP MOVING AND STAY ON YOUR TOES!** A good goalie's feet are constantly moving and ready for anything that's coming their way. Never sit back on your heels, that's when you'll make mistakes.

2 **SHOUT... LOUD!** You have to communicate with your team, let them know when you need help or when you think they need to be watching opposing players.

3 **STAY LOOSE AND RELAXED.** If you're tense, diving and getting hit with the ball will hurt more.

4 **STAY AWAKE!** You've got to be watching the game all the time in order to be ready to step up when it's your turn to shine. Remember, it only takes seconds for the game to change completely.

5 **WATCH PLAYERS' FEET.** The way their feet are positioned when going to take a kick can indicate where the ball is going.

6 **BOUNCE BACK!** After diving your length for a ball, recover quickly, play doesn't stop because you're on the ground.

7 **STAY SQUARE TO THE BALL.** At all times, keep your hips and shoulders pointed towards the shooter.

8 **TREAT ALL SHOTS WITH RESPECT!** No matter how soft the shot or how easy the save, always make the effort to get the ball under full control. It's when you get lazy that mistakes happen.

9 **HAVE AN INSURANCE POLICY!** Always have a part of your body behind the ball as well as your hands. That way, if the ball slips through your fingers, your body will be there to stop it.

10 **HAVE COURAGE!** Take pride in your position as your team's last defender and have confidence in yourself. You have to put yourself in positions where you might end up getting hit but it's these saves that win matches.

MARK SCHWARZER

JIM PLATT

Boro *Legends*

George Camsell

Camsell is Middlesbrough's all-time top scorer. He recorded almost a goal a game in his 14 seasons in a Boro shirt.

His 59 goals in 1926-27 season shattered all records, only to be narrowly eclipsed by Everton's Dixie Dean a year later. A former miner from Durham City, he quickly made his mark at the club's former home of Ayresome Park. He finished with 345 goals in all competitions. He also won nine caps for England.

Graeme Souness

Souness was a powerful and skilful midfield player who starred in the 1973-74 Second Division championship side engineered by manager Jack Charlton.

The Scottish international tackled hard and possessed excellent shooting skills. He also had a fierce will to win that rubbed off on his team-mates. He went on to join Liverpool for £325,000 in January 1978 and went on to win the European Cup three times with the Reds before embarking on a successful managerial career.

Massimo Maccarone

Maccarone will always be remembered for his last-gasp goals against Basel and Steaua Bucharest that drove Boro to the UEFA Cup final in Eindhoven in 2006.

He arrived during 2002 in a club record move from Italian second division side Empoli, Steve McClaren investing £8.15m in the little striker who had impressed in the European U-21 Championships. His Boro career was mixed and he was loaned out to Parma and Siena for lengthy periods. But his UEFA Cup heroics have ensured his place in club history.

Wilf Mannion

Mannion is arguably the greatest player to have pulled on a Boro shirt. The "Golden Boy" was the complete player, a masterful dribbler and all-round entertainer.

He was also Boro's most capped player with 26 England caps until Australian goalkeeper Mark Schwarzer overhauled his record before leaving for Fulham. Mannion was part of a talented Boro team that seemed destined for major honours only for the league programme to be abandoned with the outbreak of the Second World War. He made up for lost time when fixtures resumed in 1946 and had amassed more than 350 appearances by the time he left the club in 1954.

Hendrie was an all-action player who endeared himself to Boro fans for his whole-hearted performances. He was signed by Colin Todd for £500,000 in 1990 and picked up a Second Division championship medal with Leeds.

His elevation to cult status came under Todd's successor, Lennie Lawrence. He reverted to a central striking role and the goals began to flow. He became club captain during 1993-94 and was among the country's top scorers in the early part of the season. He also scored both goals in a 2-1 win over Luton in the last-ever competitive match at Ayresome Park, ensuring Boro lifted the First Division championship.

John Hendrie

Colin Cooper

Cooper was the mainstay of Bruce Rioch's double promotion-winning side in the late 1980s before following the manager to Millwall.

His career flourished after a move to Nottingham Forest, where he won two England caps. Cooper returned to Boro in 1998 and again established himself as a crowd favourite as he defied the advancing years with his tireless commitment to the cause. He is now a first-team coach under manager Gareth Southgate.

3 ...is the magic number

Stewart Downing

v Manchester City

PREMIER LEAGUE, MAY 2008

Downing's copybook volley with the outside of his left foot bent beyond the reach of City 'keeper Isaksson in our never-to-be-forgotten 8-1 win on the final day of the season.

Joseph-Desire Job

v Sporting Lisbon

UEFA CUP, MARCH 2005

"There's only one job on Teesside!" So sang the Boro faithful after seeing the Cameroon striker produce an awesome overhead kick. Incredibly, Job barely celebrated scoring one of the Riverside's greatest ever goals as Boro had been three down at the time.

Massimo Maccarone

v Steaua Bucharest

UEFA CUP, APRIL 2006

"Boro have struck a stake through the heart of Dracula's boys!" yelled an ecstatic Alastair Brownlee as perhaps the Riverside's most unforgettable goal completed an astonishing comeback and sent Maccarone and co into the UEFA Cup final. The Italian met Stewy Downing's left-wing cross with a perfect header that had 'goal' written all over it.

L

LEROY Lita

MIDDLESBROUGH Mastermind

In what year was Middlesbrough Football Club formed?

1. ____________

Which season did Gareth Southgate win Boro's Player of the Year?

2. ____________

What year was the Riverside Stadium built?

3. ____________

Who did Boro beat in the Carling Cup Final 2004?

4. ____________

What is Jimmy Floyd Hasselbaink's real first name?

5. ____________

Who did Boro play in the opening game of the 2009-10 season?

6. ____________

As the crow flies, who have been Boro's nearest league rivals?

7. ____________

What is Boro's training ground called?

8. ____________

How much did Boro pay for then record signing, Massimo Maccarone?

9. ____________

Which Boro star was known as 'the Guv'nor'?

10. ____________

POSITIVELY CHARGED Nucleus

Behind Gareth Southgate is a dedicated team of coaches and medical staff

THE COACHES

Gareth Southgate is supported by an experienced team of coaches made up of Colin Cooper, Steve Agnew, Steve Pears and Martin Scott.

Cooper enjoyed two successful spells at the club as a player. He also played for Nottingham Forest and Millwall. The highlight of his career was to win two England caps.

Agnew was a cultured midfielder who starred for Sunderland, Blackburn, Leicester, Barnsley and York City. He has also had previous coaching experience at Hartlepool, where he was assistant manager, and Leeds.

Pears was one of the club's most famous goalkeepers who was between the posts in the mid-1980s when the side that Bruce Rioch built won two promotions to the old First Division. He coaches the Boro keepers including Brad Jones, Danny Coyne, Jason Steele and Connor Ripley.

Scott enjoyed his best playing days with Sunderland and was part of Peter Reid's legendary promotion team in the mid-1990s. After management experience at Hartlepool, he joined Boro initially as a youth coach but now looks after the reserves.

THE MEDICAL TEAM

Head of Medical Grant Downie is supported by physiotherapists Adam Reed and Trevor Langford. As well as helping injured players return to action, they also advise them on how to prevent injuries.

IN CHARGE OF FITNESS

Conditioning coach Nick Allamby makes sure the players stay fit and consults with the manager about the weekly training sessions and matchday preparation.

FOOTBALL CONSULTANT

Former Crystal Palace manager Alan Smith works closely with the manager on all football matters.

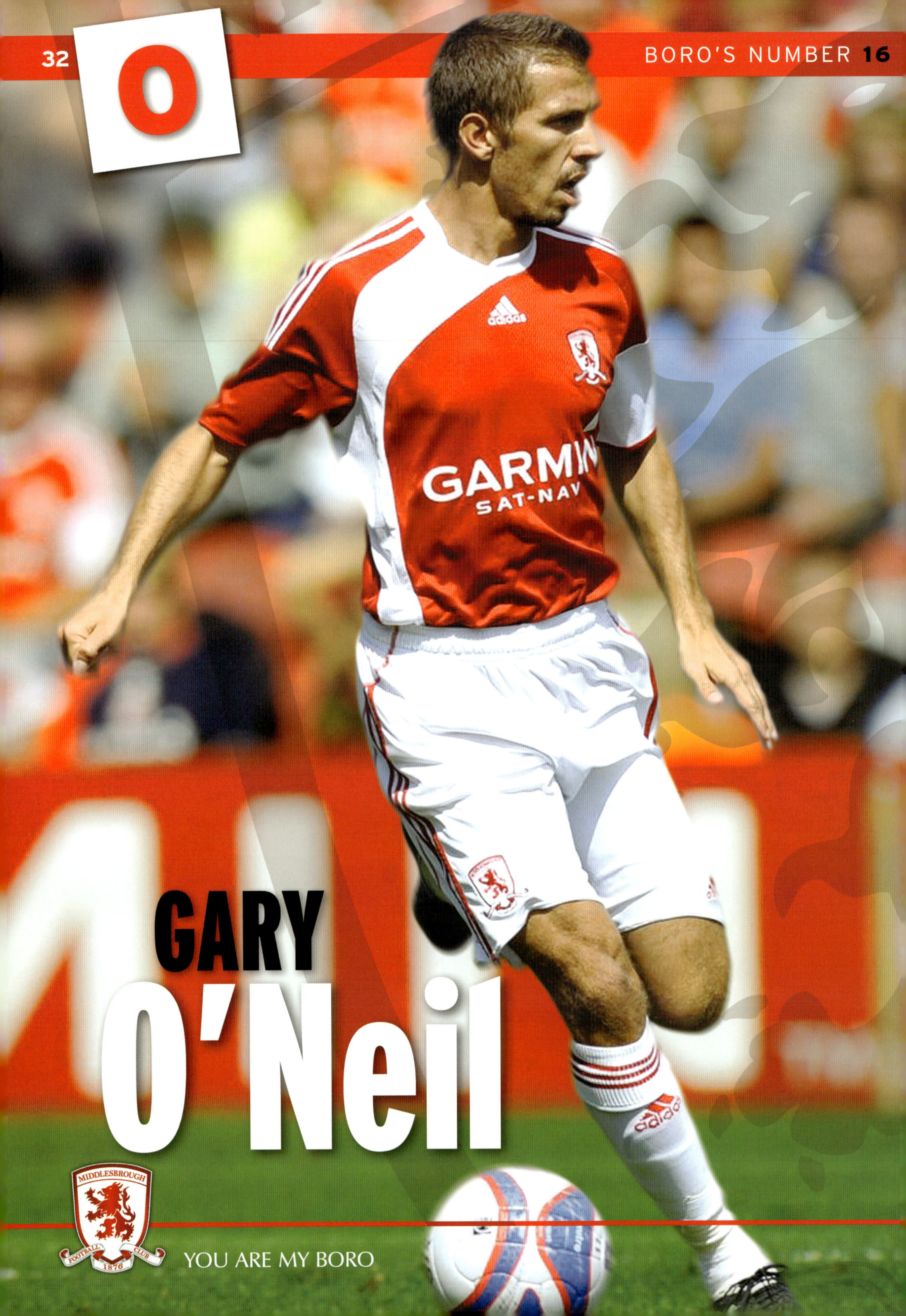

GARY O'Neil

P

Can you finish this picture of Gary O'Neil and colour it in?

PICTURE Perfect

PLAYER OF THE YEAR

Once a year the Club votes for the player who has showed outstanding skill and dedication, and who has really had an impact on the team's performance to be the Player of the Year. This special honour is reserved for only the best.

Have you got what it takes?

RULES

- You need a dice and a counter for each player
- The youngest player begins
- Place all counters near the first circle
- Throw the dice to move your counter across the board
- If your counter lands on an action field, follow the instructions
- Whoever reaches the end of the board first is...

PLAYER OF THE YEAR!

Booked for celebrating a goal with the fans
MOVE BACKWARD TWO SPACES

Your progress earns you a call-up to the National team
MOVE FORWARD THREE SPACES

Getting tired towards the end of the season
MISS A TURN

YOU MADE IT! YOU ARE VOTED
PLAYER OF THE YEAR!

Your hat-trick puts the Club Top of the League
MOVE FORWARD TWO SPACES

The coach praises your dedication and team spirit
MOVE FORWARD ONE SPACE

You miss a couple of games because of injury
MISS A TURN

Your latest goal is voted 'Goal of the Month'
MOVE FORWARD ONE SPACE

You are fouled badly and need to be carried off
MOVE BACKWARD ONE SPACE

Quick fire

JULIO ARCA

Favourite Music?
R&B

Favourite TV Programme?
Documentaries

Favourite Film?
Casino

Favourite Computer Game?
Pro-evolution

Favourite Food?
Japanese

Favourite Drink?
Red Wine

Favourite Car?
Bentley Continental

Favourite Holiday?
Caribbean

JUSTIN HOYTE

Favourite Music?
R&B

Favourite Food?
Mum & Dad's Cooking

Favourite Drink?
Sun Exotic, Pineapple & Coconut

Favourite Film?
An American Film called Life

Favourite TV Programme?
Entourage

Favourite Computer Game?
Pro-evolution

Favourite Car?
SLR McLaren

Favourite Holiday?
Maldives

JONATHAN GROUNDS

Best player in the world?
Messi

Best game played in?
Debut v Liverpool

Advice for aspiring young players?
Always work hard

Who is your best friend in football?
David Wheater

Who is the joker in the dressing room?
Tony Mac

Which superpower would you like to have?
Invisibility

Theme song for yourself?
Michael Jackson - Beat It

ADAM JOHNSON

First thing you do in the morning?
Press snooze!

Any hidden talents?
Golf - not really, I'm awful

If not a footballer what would you be?
A model

Describe yourself in 3 words?
Outgoing, Intelligent, Loud

Person you'd like to meet?
Tiger Woods

One wish?
Win the World Cup with England

PENALTY PRIDE

STAGE 1
EASY PEASY

1 All you need is a football and some cones to mark out a goal

2 Take ten steps back and practice shooting into different parts of the goal

3 Aim for different parts of the goal so that every penalty is different

STAGE 2
MEDIUM

1 Ask a friend to join you

2 Tell your friend where you are going to put your shot, then go for it

3 This makes it more of a challenge and so helps you improve

STAGE 3
TOUGH

1 Ask your friend to go in goal, now you've got to score past a goalie

2 Shout where you're aiming for and go for it again

3 Use the side of your foot for accuracy, or the top for power

STAGE 4
PRO

1 Now you're ready for a penalty shoot-out

2 Ask some mates to join in and one of you has to go in goal

3 Take five penalties each and see who comes out on top!

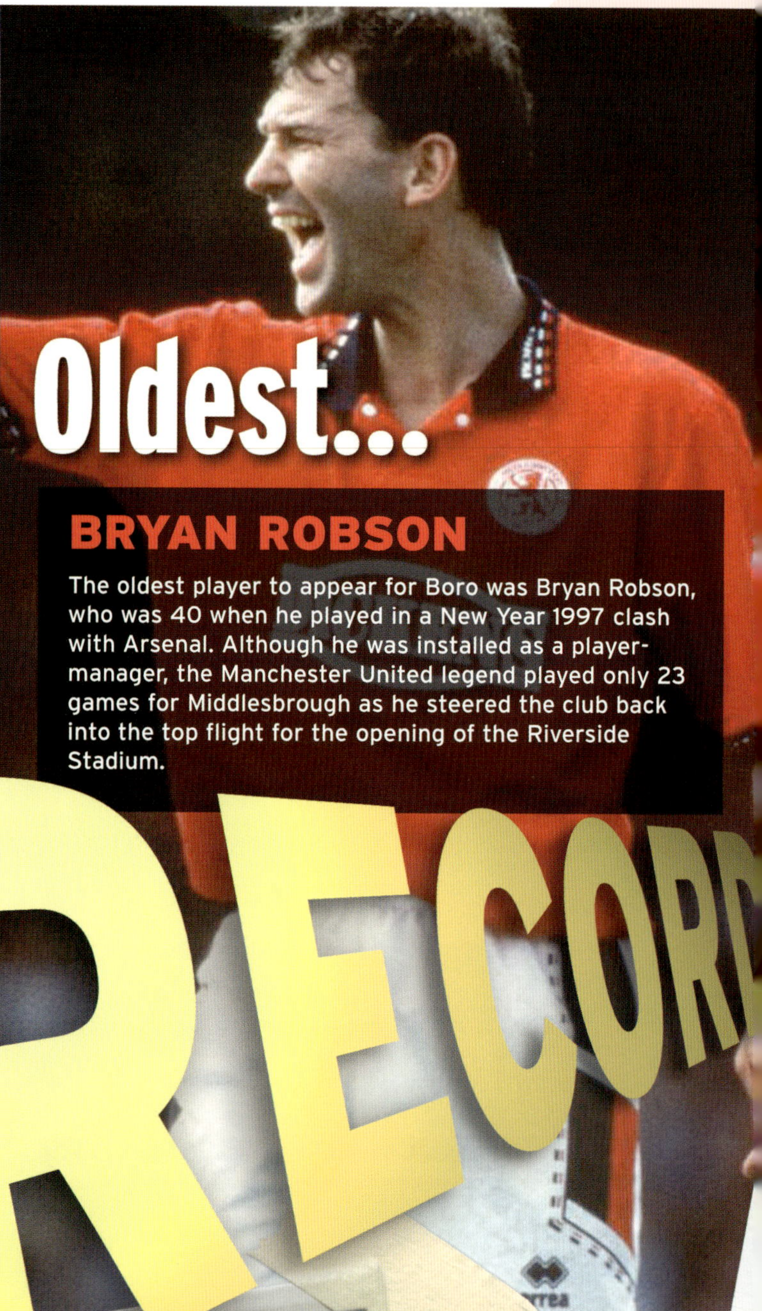

Oldest...

BRYAN ROBSON

The oldest player to appear for Boro was Bryan Robson, who was 40 when he played in a New Year 1997 clash with Arsenal. Although he was installed as a player-manager, the Manchester United legend played only 23 games for Middlesbrough as he steered the club back into the top flight for the opening of the Riverside Stadium.

Youngest...

RECORD

ANDY CAMPBELL

The youngest player to appear for Boro in the Premier League was Andy Campbell, who became the first 16-year-old to appear in the Premiership when he made his debut against Sheffield Wednesday in April 1996. Never a regular, Campbell moved to Cardiff City for £950,000 in 2002 and now plays in non-league football.

One of the tallest players to appear for Boro was Mark Schwarzer at 6ft 5ins. The Australian international was Boro first choice for a decade before his free transfer to move to Fulham in summer 2008.

During that time he made well over 400 appearances for the club and helped them win the Carling Cup in 2004.

BREAKERS

Tallest...

JUNINHO

One of the shortest players to have played for Boro was Juninho. Although he was only 5ft 4ins, Juninho stands tall in Middlesbrough history as one of the club's greatest players.

He enjoyed three spells with the club he first joined from Sao Paulo in 1995.

Shortest!

Boro's TOP FIVE

BORO 4 Steaua Bucharest 2

UEFA Cup semi-final 2nd leg
April 27 2006

This was a night that Boro fans' dreams are made of! For the second time in three weeks, all seemed lost with Boro trailing 3-0 on aggregate - and we all know that lightning doesn't strike twice, don't we? Wrong!

A battling first leg display in Romania had left Boro trailing by just a single goal and on the verge of our first European final. It all went wrong in the first 23 minutes as Boro went two goals behind on the night and three on aggregate. Surely the dream of a small town in a European final was over.

Massimo Maccarone began the fight-back with a low drive before half time before the inspirational Mark Viduka headed home Stewart Downing's left-wing cross to level the scores on the night. Boro fans started to believe that the impossible could be possible yet again when Chris Riggott leveled the aggregate scores - but still Boro trailed on the away goals rule. Still another goal was needed. That goal finally came in the 89th minute as Steaua's wilting defence gave way for a fourth time. Downing beat his marker on the left before swinging in another inch-perfect cross and achieved his third assist of the half as Maccarone powered home a fantastic diving header to send the Riverside into raptures.

Boro were on their way to Eindhoven - and in the words of Boro commentator Alastair Brownlee "Party! Party! Party! Everyone round my house for a Parmo!"

2 BORO 4-1 Basel UEFA Cup quarter final 2nd leg · April 6 2006

A match that fans rightly claimed was the greatest in Boro's history - for exactly three weeks! Boro made the Swiss roll as Steve McClaren's side fought their way back from three goals down to win in one of the most unbelievable comebacks of all-time. Trailing 2-0 from the first leg in Switzerland, Boro looked dead and buried when they conceded again after just 22 minutes - but that only served to kick-start a performance of passion, belief and drama. Mark Viduka began the comeback with goals either side of half-time before strike partner Jimmy Floyd Hasselbaink blasted in a third with 12 minutes remaining. The spectacular comeback was complete in the 90th minute when Massimo Maccarone fired home to send Boro fans into ecstasy.

3 BORO 6-0 Sunderland Division One · March 28 1936

It's always special when Boro beat their northeast neighbours. It's special too when we beat the reigning champions. So imagine how good it felt to beat title-holders and league leaders Sunderland by SIX goals! Flying winger Ralph Birkett scored twice for Boro, with his fellow England international George Camsell also finding the net as Boro powered into a five-goal lead before the dismissal of two Sunderland players and a late sixth to complete a truly magnificent Boro performance.

4 BORO 2-0 Liverpool Coca-Cola Cup semi-final 2nd leg · Feb 18 1998

A night remembered by Boro fans lucky enough to be there as one of the greatest ever Riverside atmospheres. The Riverside's flag-waving frenzy saw Bryan Robson's First Division team come from 2-1 behind in the first leg to storm into a 3-2 aggregate lead as early as the fourth minute, with Paul Merson scoring from the penalty spot before Italian Marco Branca made a dream start to his Boro career with a debut goal.

5 BORO 3-3 Chesterfield FA Cup semi-final · April 13 1997

Perhaps the greatest FA Cup game of all-time? This was the game that had everything - apart from a Boro victory! Minnows Chesterfield raced into a two-goal lead before 10-man Boro fought back to force extra-time, go in front through defender Gianluca Festa, only to see their Second Division opponents equalise with virtually the last touch of the game. Thankfully, Boro won the replay 3-0.

STRIKING IT RICH

...but it's more about guts than glory

JEREMIE ALIADIERE

You have to put in the legwork to reap the benefits so here we give you some top tips for becoming a striker supreme.

1 **WORK HARD!** Play your heart out right up until the final whistle, you never know when that perfect cross will come your way.

2 **PASS THE BALL!** The object is for the team to score, not the individual, if someone else has a better opportunity, help them to take it.

3 **DON'T SACRIFICE ACCURACY FOR POWER!** No matter how hard you kick the ball, if a shot isn't on target, it's never going in.

4 **FOLLOW THROUGH!** Strike the ball with the laces of your boot and don't stop your leg motion once you've connected with the ball. If you swing your leg through it will give you more momentum.

5 **KEEP SHOTS LOW AND AIM FOR THE CORNERS!** These are the hardest areas for the goalie to protect.

6 **PRACTISE MAKES PERFECT!** Practise shooting at a small target like a pole or tree to improve your accuracy, you can gradually increase your distance from the object. Soon you'll be scoring from 25 yards!

7 **ATTACK AT EVERY CHANCE YOU GET!** Make the defensive team work, the more shots you have on target, the more likely you are to score.

8 **BE PATIENT!** Don't just shoot because the ball's at your feet, wait for chances, don't waste them.

9 **WORK ON BOTH FEET!** Practise shooting with both your strong and weak foot, this will help make you a good all-round player, the more skilled you are, the more opportunities will present themselves.

10 **HAVE CONFIDENCE IN YOURSELF!** If you get a chance, take it, if you think you can take your defender, go for it! Think fast and be decisive if you want to out-fox your opponent.

JIMMY FLOYD HASSELBAINK

BRIAN CLOUGH

S

The centre of the ball is in one of the squares. ...but which one?

Spot the Ball

ANSWERS ON PAGE 62

...getting Shirty

ANSWERS ON PAGE 62

6

Six Pack

Aliadiere jubilant after scoring Boro's third goal, his second, against Ipswich Town

Adam Johnson celebrates with team mates Julio Arca and Gary O'Neil after scoring his second goal against Sheffield Wednesday at Hillsborough

The team celebrate the first goal against Doncaster

Jeremie Aliadiere scoring his first against Ipswich

Gary O'Neil celebrates his goal against Ipswich with Rhys Williams

Leroy Lita whips off his shirt as he celebrates scoring Boro's second goal against Doncaster

LOOK WHO'S TALKING

Who is the best player in the world?
Christiano Ronaldo

What is the best game you've played in?
My debut for Australia against Japan in a World Cup qualifier in front of 70,000 in Melbourne

A word of advice for aspiring youngsters?
Take sacrifices

Who is your best friend in football?
Brad Jones

Who is the joker in the dressing room?
Tony McMahon for the stupid comments he makes!

Which superpower would you like to have?
To be able to fly, so I could go home to see my family in Australia

If you were to choose a theme song for yourself what would it be?
Do You Come from a Land Down Under?

7

Boro's most famous number seven is...

One of the club's leading post-war goalscorers, he topped the goal charts for six successive seasons between 1986 and 1991. He was also a very consistent player who rarely missed a game.

Slaven began his career at a small Scottish club, Albion Rovers. Boro took him on a trial and quickly gave him a contract after he impressed in reserve games.

He came into his own during the Division Two promotion season of 1987-88 and never looked back. Slaven's tally of 15 goals in Division One in 1988-89 was bettered by only Alan Smith and John Aldridge.

Bernie kept on scoring goals until the early 1990s when he moved on to Port Vale and later Darlington. He also broke into the Republic of Ireland side, winning seven caps.

BERNIE Slaven

8

...eight differences between these pictures.

Can you spot them all?

SPOT THE Difference

ANSWERS ON PAGE 62

U

Imagine the ultimate Boro player - well here he is!

Over the years Boro fans have seen some of the greatest players in the game and we thought we'd take their best qualities and mould them together in one world-beating, Middlesbrough megastar! So here are our thoughts on how to make up the ultimate Boro payer. But do you agree?

ULTIMATE

BRAINS
GARETH SOUTHGATE

Stylish and reliable in the centre of defence, Gareth Southgate was also well known as one of the most articulate players in the game. As Boro captain and a regular England international, Gareth was always happy to give his views on the game to the waiting media after the final whistle. His intelligence was also evident out on the pitch, where he became the first Boro captain to lift a major trophy, the Carling Cup in 2004.

YOUR CHOICE

PASSION
JUNINHO

What Juninho lacked in inches he more than made up for in skill, speed and sheer love of the game. The tiny Brazilian won over the Boro fans with his scintillating displays and also his passion for the shirt. No matter how many times opponents chopped him down, Juni would spring back to his feet and run at their terrified defences all over again. No wonder the World Cup winner is Boro's most popular player of all time.

YOUR CHOICE

STRENGTH
TONY MOWBRAY

It has to be Boro's very own Captain Fantastic, Tony Mowbray. Powerful, brave and unbeatable in the air, Saltburn-born Mogga just refused to give up and would have run through brick walls for the Boro cause. Described by a TV commentator as looking like a football star from a 1930s cigarette card, his manager Bruce Rioch said that if he flew a rocket to the moon he would want Tony beside him in the passenger seat.

YOUR CHOICE

RIGHT FOOT
WILF MANNION

One of the most skilful players ever, Wilf Mannion was known as the Golden Boy of football. A star with Boro, England and even Great Britain, South Bank-born Wilf won 26 caps for his country - and it would have been more if it wasn't for World War 2! Lethal with his right from inside or outside the box, Wilf was also surprisingly good in the air for such a small man. In all he played 368 Boro games, scoring 110 goals - most of them with that wonderful right foot.

YOUR CHOICE

LAYER

HAIR
EMERSON

Emerson was not only distinctive for his silky samba style of football, but who could forget that trademark mop of curls? Brazilian midfielder Emo would regularly feint one way and send his hair and the defenders with him before darting off in the other direction and unleashing another unstoppable shot goalwards.

YOUR CHOICE

VISION
BOBBY MURDOCH

Bobby Murdoch was coming to the end of his career when he joined Boro on a free transfer in 1973, having won the European Cup with Celtic. But he proved to be the final piece in the jigsaw for manager Jack Charlton, whose Boro team romped to promotion as champions. Bobby laid on endless passes as the linkman between attack and defence, able to read the game and spot runs before delivering the ball to perfection.

YOUR CHOICE

HANDS
DANNY COYNE

With four clean sheets in his first four league games for Boro, Danny Coyne equalled a club record for shutouts at the start of a season. Last season he kept 20 clean sheets for previous club Tranmere Rovers, winning the Golden Gloves award in the process. Reliable and brave, Danny isn't the biggest of keepers but his safe hands would be ideal for our ultimate player.

YOUR CHOICE

FITNESS
GARY O'NEIL

The term midfield dynamo could have been coined for Gary O'Neil. Signed from Portsmouth for £5m, Gary has been described by Gareth Southgate as one of the fittest players at the club. Whether he plays wide or in the centre of the midfield, whoever is up against Gary is guaranteed to have a busy afternoon as he gives 110 per cent for his team from the first whistle to the last.

YOUR CHOICE

LEFT FOOT
STEWART DOWNING

If it hadn't been for a serious knee injury suffered while training with England during a trip to the USA, Stewart Downing would probably have beaten Wilf Mannion's record of 26 England caps while a Boro player. As it is he managed 23 before his £12m move to Aston Villa in summer 2009. Born in Middlesbrough's Pallister Park, Downing's chief attribute was a wand of a left foot that set up the goals in Boro's famous UEFA Cup semi-final win over Steaua Bucharest.

YOUR CHOICE

V

Four stages to the **perfect volley...**

STAGE 1
EASY PEASY

1. All you need is a football and a patch to practise in
2. Drop the ball, let it bounce, then volley it back into your hands
3. Once you start to get the hang of it, try to volley the ball without it bouncing

STAGE 2
MEDIUM

1. Ask a friend to join you and find a bit more space to play in
2. Volley the ball to your friend so they can catch it, they then volley it back to you
3. Kick it with the side or top of your foot, also try volleying without a bounce

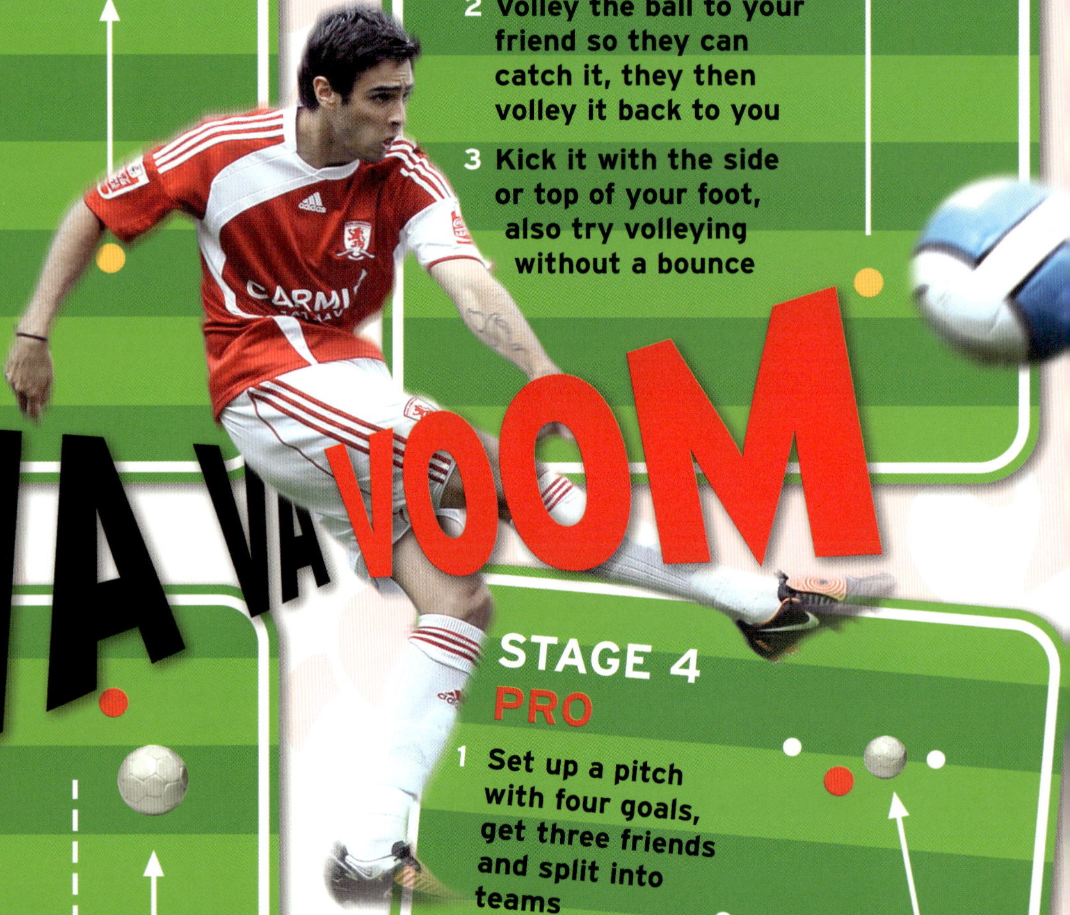

VA VA VOOM

STAGE 3
TOUGH

1. Stand a bit further apart this time and your friend starts with the ball
2. Your friend throws the ball to you and you volley it back into their hands
3. Keep practising with the top or side of your foot, swap round after five tries

STAGE 4
PRO

1. Set up a pitch with four goals, get three friends and split into teams
2. Your team mate throws you the ball and you have to score in one of the other goals
3. You win a letter every time you score a goal. First team to spell 'va va voom' wins!

DRESSED UP TO THE Nines

Boro Stars, past and present, strut their stuff on the catwalk all in the aid of charity at Middlesbrough's annual fashion show...

ADAM JOHNSON

JOSH WALKER

FASHION Strikes

LEGEND GARY PALLISTER

CRAIG HIGGNET

DAVID WHEATER

TONY McMAHON

JUSTIN HOYTE

in aid of

WE ARE MACMILLAN. CANCER SUPPORT

W

We asked six Boro stars...

If you could go to any sporting event, other than football, what would it be?

JULIO ARCA
NBA BASKETBALL

JUSTIN HOYTE
NBA ALL STAR GAME

ANDREW TAYLOR
BOXING IN VEGAS

ADAM JOHNSON
SUPERBOWL

WORLD OF SPORT

JONATHAN GROUNDS
SUPERBOWL

TONY McMAHON
US OPEN GOLF

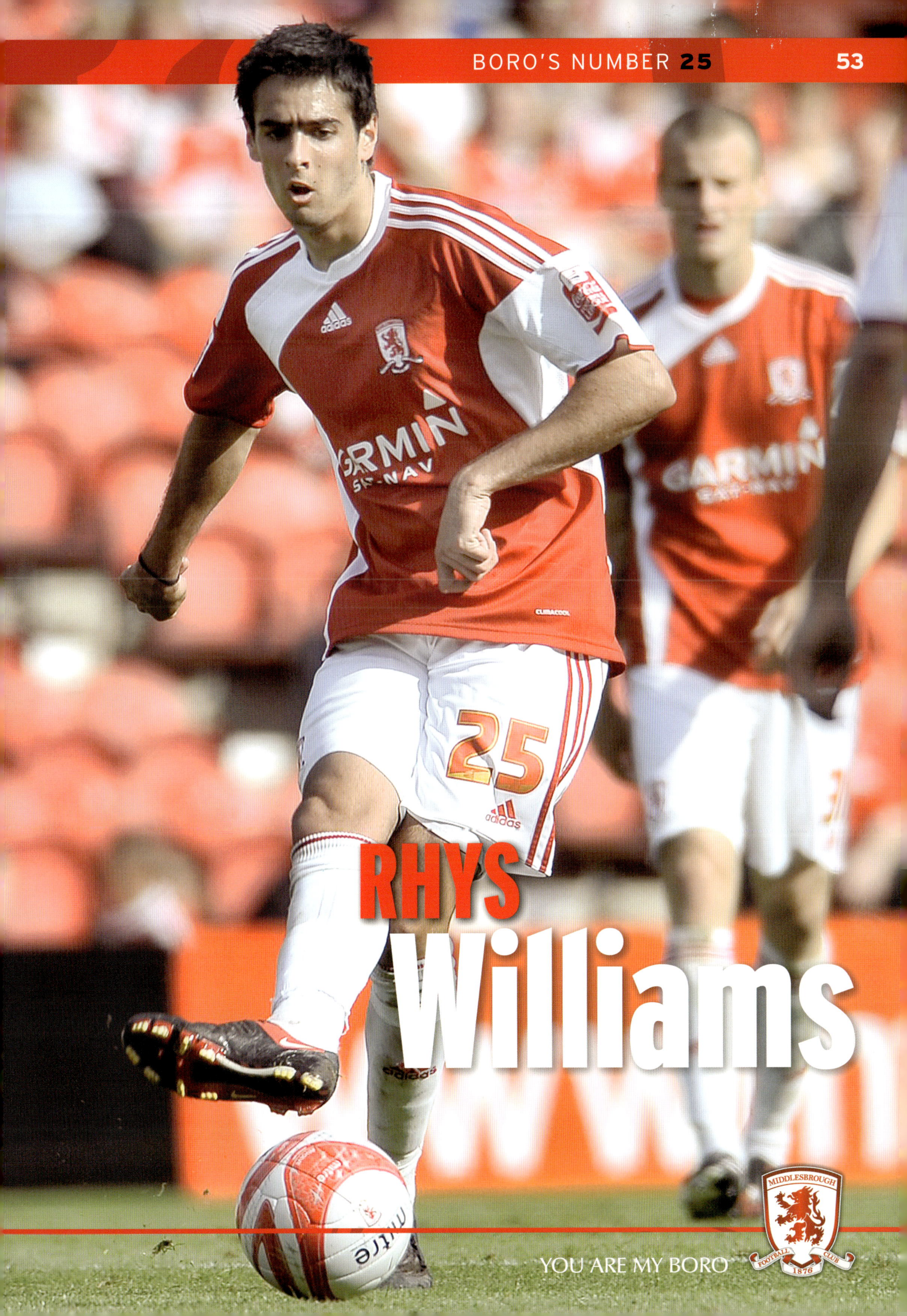

RHYS
Williams

WHO ARE YER

A

- He was born in Perth, Australia
- He has been to Burnley on loan
- He represented Wales at U21 level
- He signed his first professional contract with Boro in July 2007
- He made his full Australian debut against Japan, in June 2009

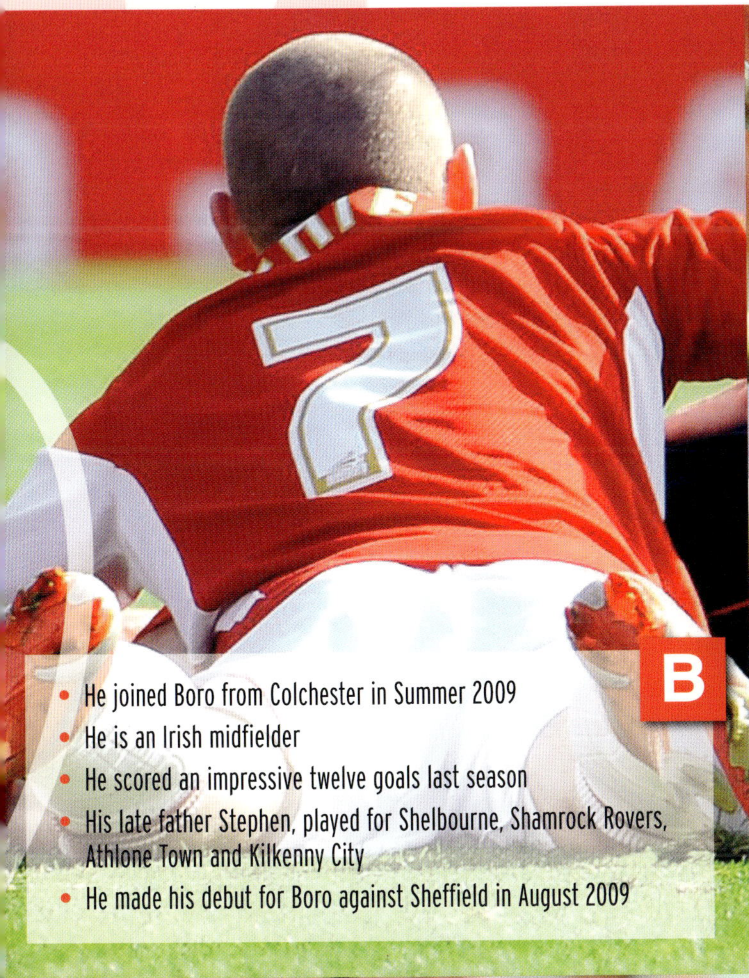

B

- He joined Boro from Colchester in Summer 2009
- He is an Irish midfielder
- He scored an impressive twelve goals last season
- His late father Stephen, played for Shelbourne, Shamrock Rovers, Athlone Town and Kilkenny City
- He made his debut for Boro against Sheffield in August 2009

C

- He signed for Middlesbrough in August 2007
- He is from Bromley, England
- He captained the England U21 team
- His middle name is Paul
- He was Portsmouth's player of the Year in 2005-2006

D

- His middle name is Andrés
- He broke a bone in his foot against Reading in August 2006
- He used to play for Sunderland
- He was born in Argentina
- He was Argentina's U21 captain

E

- He was born in Horden, England
- He is a left winger but can also play on the right wing
- He is a key member of the England U21 team
- He graduated from Middlesbrough's Academy into the first team
- He made his first team debut in 2005 against Sporting Lisbon

X These four youngsters certainly have the X-Factor

JONATHAN GROUNDS

Strong and consistent defender Jonathan began the 2007-08 season as Boro's Reserve team skipper and soon found himself playing against the likes of Steven Gerrard and Fernando Torres.

Born in Thornaby, he came through the club's youth system and can also play at left-back, centre-back or on the left side of midfield.

Jonathan gained valuable experience on loan to Norwich in the Championship last season and began the current campaign as Boro's regular left-back, keeping out England U-21 international Andrew Taylor.

A bright future is forecast for this tall, agile and brave England youth international keeper from Newton Aycliffe.

Standing 6ft 3ins tall, Jason joined Boro when he was 13 and has represented his country at U-16, U-17, U-19 and U-20 level.

He signed a new, three-year Boro contract in May 2009 and was a regular on the bench for the first team during Brad Jones' absence through injury at the beginning of this season.

Confident and capable, Jason is being tipped to make a name for himself with both club and country.

JASON STEELE

X FAC

JOE BENNETT

Promising left-sided player Joe is pushing for a regular first team squad place after coming through the Academy.

Born and brought up in Rochdale, Joe signed his first professional contract with the club in summer 2008 and is comfortable playing anywhere on the left, although he usually operates as a left-back. He made his first team debut away to West Ham United in the final game of the 2008-09 season and he was handed a new, three-year deal in August 2009.

Skilful and exciting, Joe is definitely a name to watch out for this season.

TOR

An attacking wide midfielder or forward, Stockton-born Jonathan has represented England at youth level. He was rewarded with a professional contract in 2009 after a number of impressive performances for both club and country.

He made his first team debut away to West Ham United in the final game of the 2008-09 campaign and has been a regular in the squad this season.

Lightning quick and with great attitude and willingness to learn, Jonathan has all the attributes for a career at the top.

JONATHAN FRANKS

10 ...things you didn't know about Boro

There were originally two teams in Middlesbrough - Middlesbrough and Ironopolis - but only the team we now know at Boro survived.

Boro once had four brothers from the same family on their books. The Carr bothers - JACKY, Willie, Harry and George - all played for us in the early years of the last century.

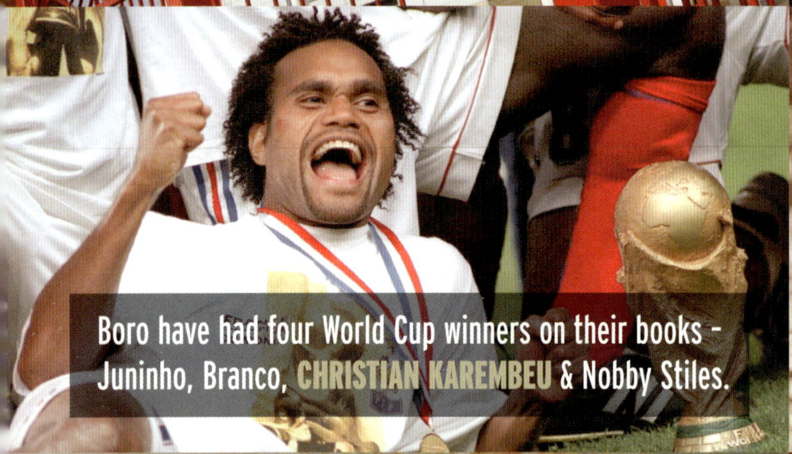

Boro have had four World Cup winners on their books - Juninho, Branco, CHRISTIAN KAREMBEU & Nobby Stiles.

David 'SPIKE' ARMSTRONG never missed a game for more than eight years from March 1972 to August 1980.

Record-breaking striker GEORGE CAMSELL hit an incredible 18 goals in nine games for England.

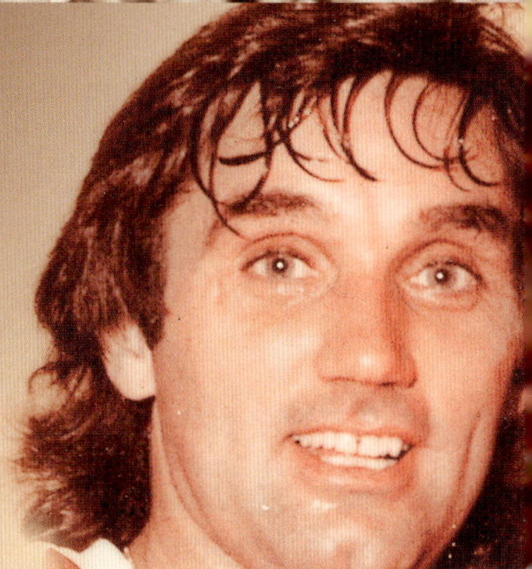

The famous GEORGE BEST once played for Boro, in a testimonial for long-serving goalkeeper Jim Platt in 1982.

GARY PALLISTER'S transfer "fee" from Billingham Town was a set of shirts. He was later sold to Man United for a British record £2.3m.

The legendary GEORGE HARDWICK is the only person to have skippered a Great Britain football team, in 1947.

Only two of STEVE McCLAREN'S signings remain on the playing staff - Emanuel Pogatetz and Chris Riggott.

Boro's old ground AYRESOME PARK witnessed one of the greatest World Cup shocks of all time when North Korea beat the mighty Italy in a 1966 group match.

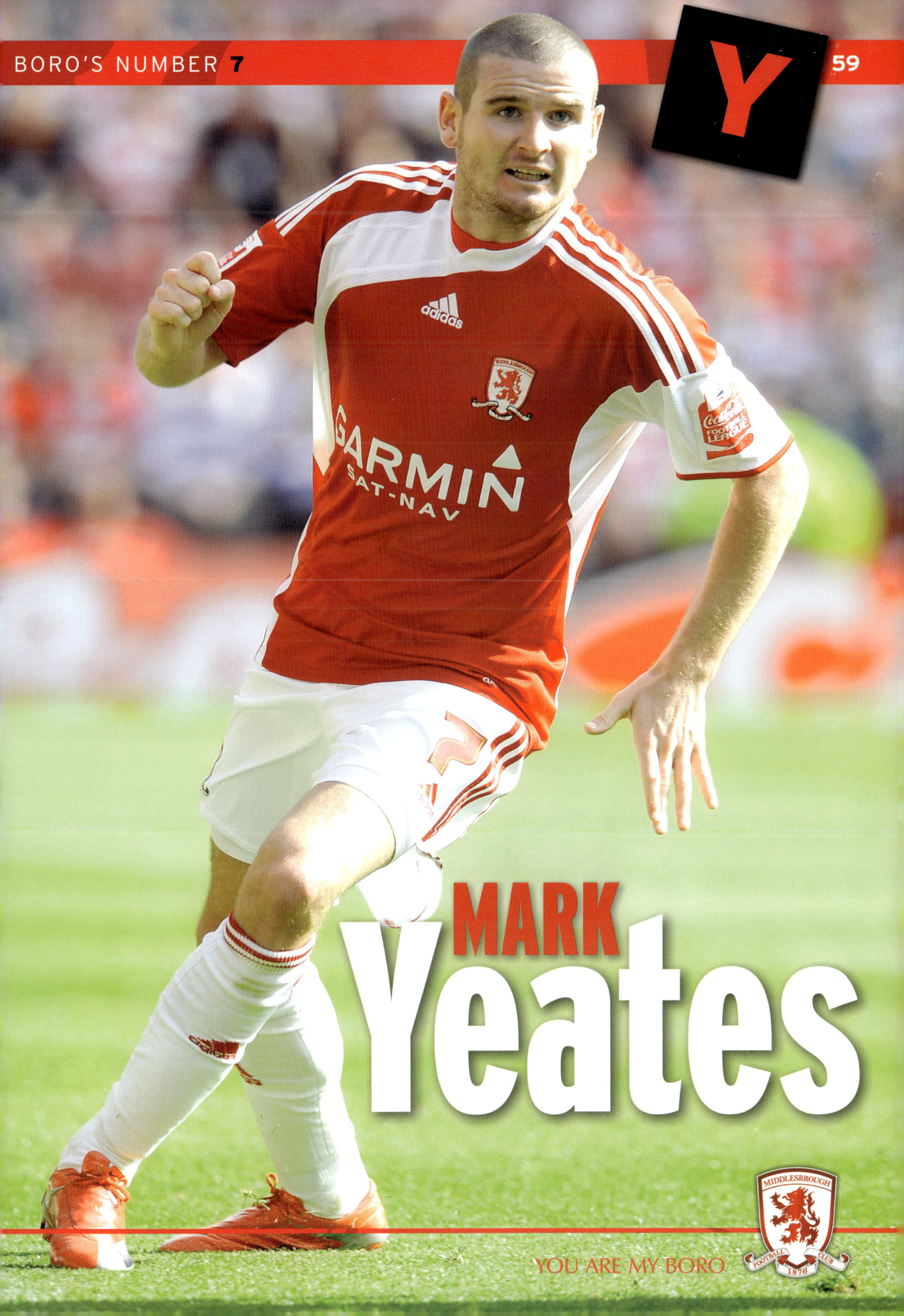

MARK Yeates

YOU ARE MY BORO

Z

Impress your mates... by going around the world!

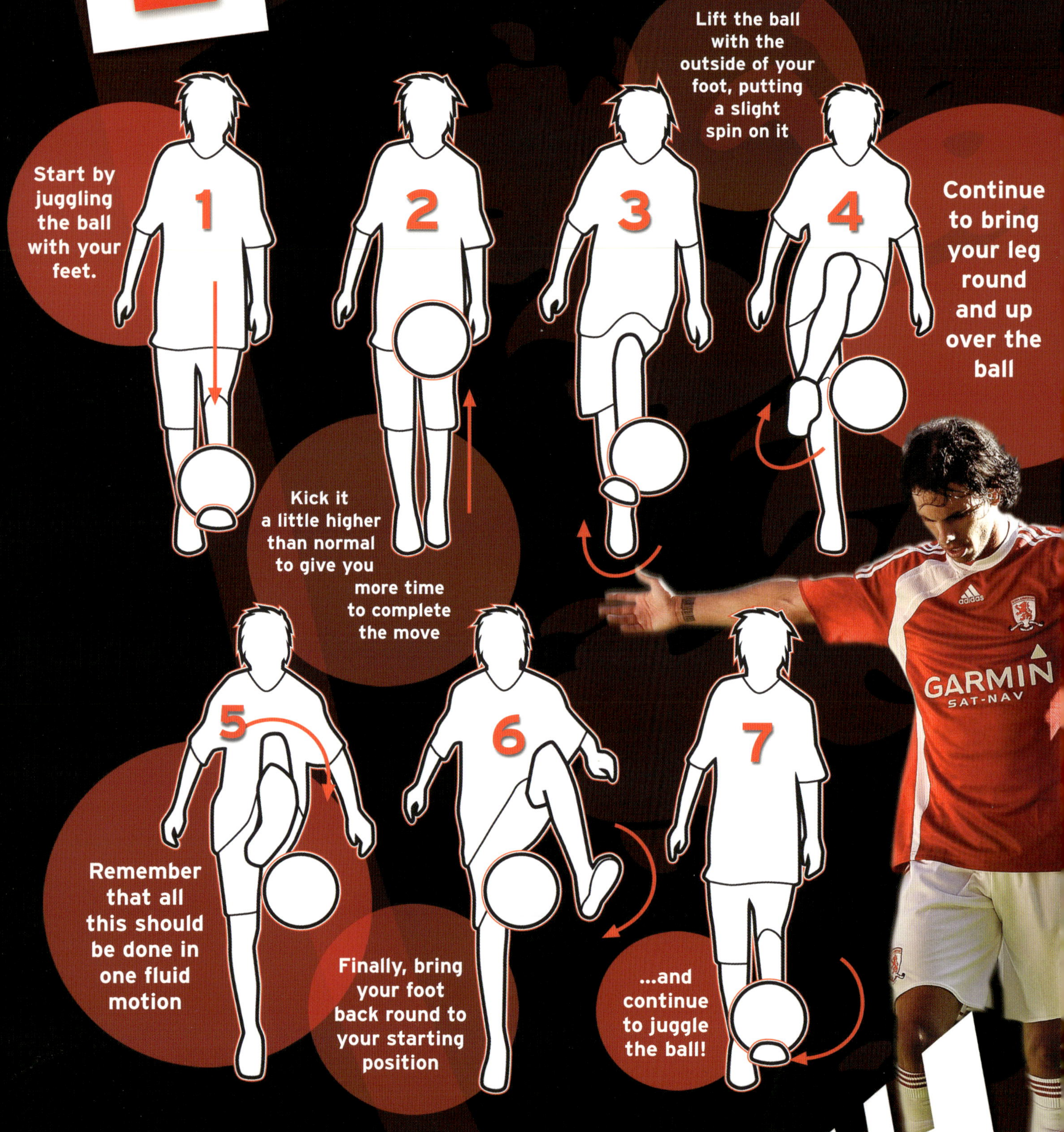

ZIGAZIGAH

eleven most capped international players

MARK SCHWARZER
AUSTRALIA

The Aussie goalkeeper played almost twice as many international games as any player throughout Boro's long history. Having played in the 2006 World Cup finals, he is now looking forward to his second World Cup in South Africa in 2010.

SZILARD NEMETH
SLOVAKIA

The striker was never a big name at the Riverside but he is Slovakia's all-time top scorer, hitting 13 goals for his country while with Boro.

WILF MANNION
ENGLAND

Nicknamed 'The Golden Boy', many people who saw Mannion play say he was the club's greatest ever star. He was an England regular immediately after World War II.

ARTHUR FITZSIMONS
REPUBLIC OF IRELAND

A regular in a Boro forward line that also included the legendary Brian Clough, Fitzsimons played for his country throughout the 1950s.

TUNCAY SANLI
TURKEY

One of the most popular Boro players of recent years, Tuncay was captain of Turkey and played a key role in their run to the semi-finals of the 2008 European Championships.

STEWART DOWNING
ENGLAND

Born in Pallister Park, Middlesbrough, Downing progressed from Boro's famous Academy to become an England regular, appearing in the 2006 World Cup finals.

EMANUEL POGATETZ
AUSTRIA

Captain of club and country, hard man defender Pogatetz has been an automatic choice for his country for many years.

ERIC McMORDIE
NORTHERN IRELAND

A boyhood friend of the famous George Best, McMordie played regularly for his country throughout the 1960s and early 1970s.

JIM PLATT
NORTHERN IRELAND

Boro's first choice goalkeeper throughout the 1970s and early 1980s, Platt played in the 1982 World Cup but would have played many more times for his country but for the brilliance of the legendary Pat Jennings.

MOHAMED SHAWKY
EGYPT

He may never have been a big success in English football, but Shawky has been an automatic choice for Egypt for many years, playing more games for his country than he has for Boro!

TERRY COCHRANE
NORTHERN IRELAND

A then club record £238,000 signing from Burnley in 1978, tricky winger Cochrane was a fans' favourite who was a regular member of an excellent Northern Ireland squad that qualified for the 1982 World Cup. Cochrane missed out through injury.

*Figures correct up to September 2009

PAGE 9: CREST TEST:

A - Leicester City. B - Derby County.
C - Barnsley. D - Ipswich Town.
E - West Bromwich Albion.
F - Sheffield Wednesday. G - Reading.
H - Sheffield United.

PAGE 14: STARS IN THEIR EYES:

A - Matthew Bates. B - Seb Hines.
C - Emanuel Pogatetz. D - Julio Arca.
E - David Wheater. F - Didier Digard.
G - Mohamed Shawky. H - Tony McMahon.

PAGE 16-17: FANTASTIC:

Clockwise from far left: Ricky Hatton, Andy Murray, Jonny Wilkinson, Fabio Capello, Andrew Flintoff.

PAGE 30: MIDDLESBROUGH MASTERMIND:

1 - 1876. 2 - 2001-02 season.
3 - 1995. 4 - Bolton Wanderers.
5 - Jerrel. 6 - Sheffield United.
7 - Hartlepool. 8 - Rockliffe Park.
9 - £8.15million. 10 - Paul Ince.

PAGE 42: SPOT THE BALL:

PAGE 43: GETTING SHIRTY:

A - Ipswich Town. B - Doncaster Rovers.
C - Sheffield United. D - Newcastle United.
E - Peterborough United. F - Crystal Palace.

PAGE 47: SPOT THE DIFFERENCE:

PAGE 54-55: WHO ARE YER?:

A - Rhys Williams. B - Mark Yeates.
C - Gary O'Neil. D - Julio Arca.
E - Adam Johnson.